MOTHER BODY

DIAMOND FORDE

Distributed by Independent Publishers Group
Chicago

Saturnalia Books
105 Woodside Rd.
Ardmore, PA 19003
info@saturnaliabooks.com

ISBN: 978-1-947817-24-1 (print) 978-1-947817-25-8 (eBook)
Library of Congress Control Number: 2020949464

Cover art by Lauren Buchness
Interior Illustrations by Diana Kitthajaroenchai
Book design by Robin Vuchnich

Distributed by:
Independent Publishing Group
814 N. Franklin St.
Chicago, IL 60610
800-888-4741

for us

Contents

BLOOD ODE

fat girl nicks herself shaving in the shower,
resents the water that will carry her
blood to sea. Blood, worthless currency,
cannot buy a country but becomes it,
platelets stitching into streets. fat girl weeps
for the blood that won't return—
how many mothers have tried
such a homecoming, sons and daughters
inking the tarry streets? fat girl becomes
a mother through her looking, has seen
too many children mangled by a sense
of justice. She carries somebody's child
in the crater their deaths create
inside her—if she could just reach deep
enough, if she could piecemeal her own
plump, how many layers would it take
to make a bulletproof lung? fat girl mourns
the blood muling a persistent path
through the drainpipes. If blood must be
taken, let there be coral glittering
like gemstones at their feet, dolphins pitching
foam in arcs out from the sea. Let there be air
enough. fat girl could be a mother, fretting
the impossible journey of her blood.

Womb Elegy

I have made you everything
a queen needs: palace and

peasant, halls kicked through—
you knelt, Mother,

burdened by giving
shape to liver, fingers, nose,

what did I take
to compose my bones?

I stole away
with natal greed, sprouted toes,

sipped the listless offerings
of womb milk

through umbilical straw.
You didn't notice this exchange

as more than nine-month-
nights wed to waiting,

but I will eat off you
even when memory's bread

leaves crumbs to gnaw on.
I'm your baby bred

from hunger, a space
if space could stretch

its fist into the rose dome
of womb. I hunger

to grow, hunger to orbit
the mother body,

hunger to body, as if
to make whole

my absence from you, I feed
another mouth my wine.

Mother like savior
and saint, likely served on silver

platter. Daughter, gnashing
with hunger. What does she want

if not certainty
of wholeness?

She, the only loss
in a uterus flush with living

tissue. Is a daughter only whole
still full of mother

blood? Then the first death
sputtering you out for air.

The second, my return
to shapelessness. God willing,

that vastness, you.

Three Lessons on the Adolescent Body

Lit by the hazy noon sputtered through our grade school panes, we file
      into the gym, squeak a thrum of rubber shoes—

what holy racket. Our voices—
      the hallowed harangue of small gods witnessing

power. We skip, indifferent to our leaping legs. Our feet
slam lacquer, scuff omens   of floorboard ash.

In a game, we build lines from linked arms, construct ourselves
      a fence to wreck
again   again.   We, children. So destructive.

So miraculous.

*

Beside me, Blonde Girl studies the field of fuzz blooming my bare arms.
We're ten. I'm a soldering gun. My elbows cinder to ash. Her mouth—
thunder and steel—teeth flickering flint—straight-razor slitting her tongue,
the click-wit in her throat unsheathes, says you should shave that, then slings
up her own skin for scrutiny—smooth-white, the belly of an airplane buffed
by clouds.

We are headed somewhere.

*

The first time I ask Momma if I can shave
she lifts her jeans, reveals
the teeming tabernacle of her own legs,
dark hairs bowed in prayer.

Trust me, sweetie, she says, no man will care,
then sees the smoldering hesitation still
coaled in my eyes, so offers to raze
my body's curls with her clipper set.

When I tell her no, it's not because I have learned
to bear my bristles, but because
to remove a part of myself feels like admitting
god made a mistake when she made me.

FOUR YEARS AFTER MY THIRD-DEGREE BURN, MY PARENTS DIVORCE
after Truong Tran

at night, darkness scored
beneath her eyes, my mother begs
my father to let her stay
with her kids keep us
from spilling tea on our spindling
hips   her kids still growing
                without her

a scar is a seam still hemming
memory to a body
my memories are cobblestones
paved on my right thigh   boiled
water bubbled my skin to scales

at day, my mother leaves
for work   she holds me
then dips her hand in the burn
cream   rubs relief on my heat
cured legs   prays skin can forgive
this absence   the gap
between what was and is

Semi-Confessions from the Poet of Wickedness
after Walt Whitman

There's a reason I've never written about you,
~~stepmother, dispelled from childhood tales,~~
I can't stand a willow to your hatchet-edged
smile, to the *drinking & breeding* nights I bunkered
in bed, waiting for your steps to rattle the rafters

to bones. ~~I want everyone to see you as the monster
you are.~~ Your fingers arc in chords inside
my throat. I choke on your fluted whispers.
Thundercloud *steeped with bitter and angry
hail*, hell-cat, crown of wayward

stars, hazy in Zinfandel clouds, you'd shot
and the spit burst cannonballs
from your mouth, the whole house splintered
and smoky, you burped, and fire roiled
its hills inside you. There are ships

sunken as dusk in your chest, and still
when you said your mother never said
she loved you, ~~I thought we shared
something: mothers with claws snagging
our childish, blooming chests, we learned~~

~~to stop whistling through the holes.~~
Once, unsteady on dream-drunk feet, you reached
for my hand, ~~waited for me to hold you~~
~~tender, new as summer grass.~~ In the stillness
my nerves echoed a scream.

There are truths that are true and truths
that are true when I tell them. ~~I wanted~~
~~to be like you, hair dipping graceful as the neck~~
~~of an anhinga, bones so light they floated~~
~~like a pear-shaped balloon.~~

THE LAST TIME YOU ARE CLOSE TO YOUR BODY

you're at the table where family dinners have to happen. Your stepmother tells you, again, that you're disgusting, this time because she caught you scrubbing panties in the bathroom like your aunt taught you when you were too poor for hygiene. Your father, who is past his past already, is not at the table and wouldn't be because this isn't family dinner. She lists all the reasons you disgust her. You are surprised she doesn't mention your mother. She mentions your mother when she wants to hurt you most; she is never without your mother on her tongue. Your mother is barbed wire hurting you both. You want to ask which part of this is wrong, but you already know it is you. It is why, when you wash your purple-printed panties in the sink, you hope the steam will swallow the mirror whole. You remember your mother in a ratty blue bathrobe, before your father was synonymous with money. Your stepmother would never wear that bathrobe, would never touch anything that feels like poverty on the palms—she will never hold you.

Looking Out my Bedroom Window in Postignano

for my half-brother

Throwing back the curtain, I let its linen nurse my hope
for the picturesque. Picture it:

hills nudging their green knees apart, dogs braying and brawling, well
on the lawn. How to paint this

accurately? Is it my imagination that slants these trees as toes
tripping the breeze? Is it your absence,

thousands of miles off in a boppie, nursing your cereal milk?
I know I mean nothing to you

yet. No more than that curved hip of road stretching the valley.
Certainly less than my bracelets,

whose metallic tin you've tongued for ten minutes, a lifetime
in baby-mind. The surprise here

is that I turn to think of you at all. That at dinner I recall the claw
of your tiny nails

tugging my jean leg up, up, though you hardly know the word,
or any word, to describe

these powerlines threading the yard. Shouldn't these fields plow joy?
Why then am I slung to the last

sweet moment we shared: bouncing a unicorn on my knee, the smile
you answered. Now,

your recalled laughter needles in regret. I have disliked you
more times than I loved you.

The night I couldn't calm your crying—how to describe it? a band saw
gutting its groan on pipes—

I let you howl on the floor because I could no longer stand your ringing.
I have tried to parse

this cruelty, reasoned it to my father, whose love I lost so long
I made it physical:

a finch perching and flouncing from one ledge to another. I couldn't love you.
I was unwilling to share

my father. No—I was jealous of what you didn't have: this history
hooking me along, casting

slants across your mother, my mountains, yourself.
I am dizzy with diagonals.

The Last Time I Saw My Grandfather

he told me he was glad I wasn't fat yet
but this time, with flesh glutinous on my arms and back,
hips spread like grain, I wax at his bedside and watch
his violeting cheeks, their bruised orchids flutter
with every labored breath, and I allow myself
to imagine what he must see: five years and my body
pours as golden-throated honey. We are breathless.
He is losing grip of the oxygen threading
his lungs. I fear I'm really here.   He rattles,
and I lean in for his last sound—a grunt, a groan,
a gospeled goodbye brittling to whispers.
He tells me he's proud of the family
he's led. I want to remind him what's left to do:
to fly with a fistful of heat, to walk on stilts,
or tell me, even once, he loves me, but I can't
hear him anymore. Only the metrical hum
of poetic lines. Ai, who said once that grief was sweet,
so sweet *you can never get enough of it,*
and I want to ask about guilt. It bubbles
fountainous and sweet, chocolate in my throat.
My grandfather traces his eyes on a fat glance
of me. I burble with luxurious sweetness,
thick and gratuitous guilt. I am guilty
because I am grateful for this last, fateful chance
to disappoint him—he, who once grazed his cold hand
across my rounding cheek and prayed for bones.

TRYING TO WRITE A MUSIC POEM

Momma sings in the kitchen,
phonic value of a few small notes
beaten out in egg wash

I try to describe the sound:
solemn sighing of a small dog
sinking to sleep. I'm afraid

to write my mother
with the pots and spitting pans.
The world has written her domestic

already, turned her clattering hand
hard against the bowl to motherly
yoke. I'm so tired of looking

at the lyrics of these lines, at Momma
twisting her wrist to whisk
the egg foam. Momma folding

dough, weaving Toni Braxton
solos through the buttery seams.
There was a time without her music

when the MS took her dead
and weighty legs, the numbness
constant, so constant, she welcomed needles

of pain. Describe the sound
of a woman hollowed and filled
with unsound nerves. Describe

the silence of a woman losing
leg rhythm. This is the way
of writing music. Searching stanzas

for symphonies, missing my mother.
Forgetting I missed my mother.
Present her anyway I can:

hips un-blued by rhythm, feet
tapping in staccato, gentle give
of her working hands.

ODE TO MAGIC

When it come to sex, don't test my skills / cuz my head game have
you head over heels, / give a nigga the chills, have him pay my bills.
—Lil Kim, "Magic Stick"

Praise for the anthem that raised me
from a makeshift mattress lumped together
by throw pillows. Basement hook-up

anthem. Anthem of block parties
posted up in a Black & Mild's hold.
Anthem to remind me there's value to my hips

in motion, my ass in motion buoys on the mist
in any dewy eye, and that summer
Momma handed me hand-me-down Jordache jeans

and I wore them to sit my denim ass in the bowl
of the neighbor boy's crotch, what did I own then
but the silver hook of desire reeling me in?

Teens gathered on the transformers till dark,
despite the heat, despite nothing between us
but the angling need to be seen as someone

not cramped six to a one-room apartment,
Momma sleeping each night beside a man
she didn't love. That summer, the neighbor boy

plucked irises from the sign outside our complex
for a chance to rest his hand on the copper
pennies of my brown, growing breasts—

I learned then all the trinkets a body
can conjure: *private jets, Tiffany silverware
sets*, a pallet in a place to call home.

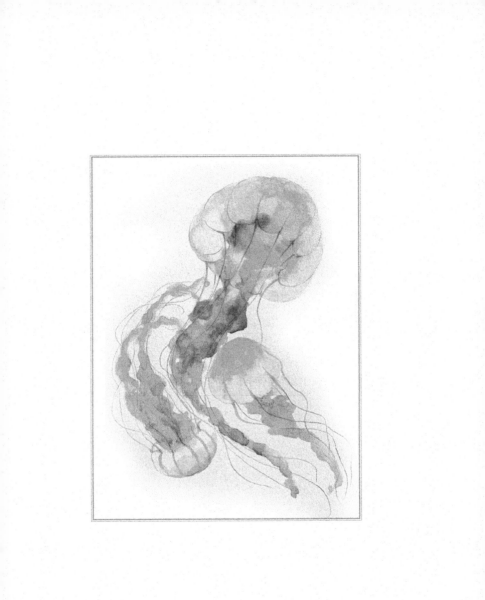

There's No Praise in Me for Me

Not even in the semi-
halo of my finger-

nails: its Byzantine
arc of gold-rose-gold,

just there. I know
the stars of my body:

constellations hot
at my hips' wide hem,

but when the light
gnaws the nectar

of my lips, I can't speak
blessings about me.

Obedience forbids self
love, and I am so good

to you. If you asked,
I would peel my skin

in strips to stitch a vest
for you. I would

altar out my spine
to worship your knees,

or crown your crown
in fingers and teeth—

look at all the good
I have to give.

What I Have to Give

The speculum, spread apart
like knees, opens
a curtain off my cervix cinema,

she swipes the film with cotton
swab, thin as memory,
then tucked in a jar, gone.

I'm here because I've forgotten
how to walk without pain
for a partner.

The gynecologist drags a swab
through my wet below,
samples what hurts

inside me, asks me to assess
my ache. I'm flightless,
pinned to the plastic slab, I shift

my feet in the stirrups
while the doctor prods parts
I'll never touch.

My periods are bad.
I do not tell her
I worship a heating pad,

my womb a false god.
I throw up. I do not
mention the smells that till

the earth in me: the rally of wild
berries at the curbside, ground beef,
my dog's sweet, powdery neck.

      She scrapes—
reminds me of my walls:
the ones I've built

from stones of Momma's voice.
Your body is a temple
and she means my body is God's

house but the doctor
isn't here for worship.
Beneath the sheet's horizon

my doctor nods, *you Black girls*
tend to suffer more
then shrugs, homing the last leg

of cotton in a tube.
My doctor has said enough
to wrap her voice's noose

on night's neck. Her words
will break silence, a laugh
track left in utero—

I will quiver on pain's needle,
a phonograph
of ceaseless screaming—

Why didn't I say something?
Like, *some nights I bleed
more than even a savior should.*

I am too much like my body.
Every visitor leaves bones
at my altar. Now, the sterile

scent of lubricant
slick between my thighs.
I pinch the sheet

and wipe, convinced
this is what I have
to give for answers.

STRIPPING

At the zoo, beneath a sky of confetti mist,
three elephants pace their own little Africa

in Alabama. Beyond the grass coughing
its last green, an unseen speaker pumps

a steady sycophantic chant behind Congo
drums. Even Ajani, the only other mammal

I've singled out, must know
this sound does not belong in the dust

beneath his feet. Desperate to unearth
this sound, Ajani grinds his tusk into the naked

husk of tree beyond him. Meanwhile,
his dick chalks circles in the dirt,

a pendulum dependent on red
earth, Ajani grunts

forward and phallic in his frenzied
bout of bark destruction. How do I tell him

they are removing the unnecessaries, too?
Or that while watching the knotted mass

of his back lift to chip, I, too, broke Ajani
to the small sum of his mating parts,

laughing at the absurdity of how quick
an elephant can break down to his dick—

would Ajani laugh, too, if he knew?
Toot a chuckle from his trumpet trunk

then slide, so smooth, his backside
against the tree behind him?

Could Ajani do what I have always
been afraid to: stand erect and baring,

the body too whole to be broken. Tell them.
Go ahead. Take exactly what you want.

HYSTERECTOMY

I joke about chucking my fat sack uterus
every period. Scramble past the bramble
of bowels with bare hands, uproot the muscular
balloon. An eviction, no more painful
than what I already feel. But I can't
remove what doesn't belong to me—

to do the violence I want
and still be loved for it.

Difficult not to be defined by motherhood—
it's all that holds me whole.
Doctors say I *might want kids one day.*
Mama prays *one day is soon.*
Curled in a helpless mess of punishment,
I let my first sin spill. This sloughed blood
a sacrifice for fantasy. My uterus,
a little home for someone else's dreams.

To do the violence I want and still be
loved for it.

"The whole is greater" means the womb
remains. Coins rattle my uterine purse,
valuable collateral for the folk I owe—
women who pray for children. Let her
have me how she wants me. Self-sacrifice
is easy. Everyone loves a martyr.

To do the violence
I want
I want
I want
and still be—

MY EX-BOYFRIEND IS A DICK JOKE

and i want to tell you that now he makes love. each low moan eroding a gravelly note in his throat. but he used to fuck. in pools and cars and backyards dotted with icy stars until the neighbors made spectacles of our bodies. now he's all wifed with generic white girl names—mary, beth, and jane—and they don't like it when you yank their hips, make milk duds of their nipples. did they moan, too, when he said he couldn't split their clit because his *nose too sensitive. dirty girl.* i make shame fit good. i wear it skin/tight. i admit that i was wild for him so i would finally be worth something. *dirty girl, i like to slide my cock in your big black pussy.* told me more than once while i tried to smash his lily lips to silence. the joke is he doesn't have a cock these days. he makes love. but i was *dirty girl.* i was *generic Black girl name.* i was *galaxy porn star.* i was *punchline.* every ounce of me—i used to dye my hair cerulean for lust. used to pretend the dark don't cut out only one of us.

Breath Ode

I have loved my breath's every elaborate shape. Sometimes, I watch it waft
its yacht on an October morning's waves. Sometimes, when winter returns,
my breath rips a rocket—no atmosphere—moon beams at my heels.

Or my breath is a magician posed with fire on her lips. She swallows
and smoke chimneys her neck till she's volcanic.
This breath tapers like a vial. That one, blooms a jellyfish

or the open mouth of a light bulb kindled to life. I pray my breath exists
in someone else someday—someone who jogs, perhaps. Or at least
someone who doesn't know what it means to cry on her 25th birthday

amazed to still have breath left to lose. I mean, breathing is a lesson
never learned, though Momma taught me to breathe slow
in the blue bar of a cop's light—*they don't understand fear*

isn't the same as guilt—but my breath is not a metaphor
so I can't shape it to a mask, to camouflage, to a bullet-proof vest.
Only my breath decides: its thrusts a dagger in my throat—

maybe my breath understands enough of living to let me end
my own damn self, but the lights hissing in my rearview leave no time
to marvel at what I guess could be my breath's last trick.

ODE TO MY NEIGHBORS

You've been a single step in the morning's wine blue,
a mechanical howl from a faucet, sizzle
of iron skillet and heat-hungry pans. The first time

I heard your muffled grunts through the walls
my chest thumped its warren of rabbits,
my fingers gripped the bed's bare edge,

then your moan, like silk pulled from the magician's
throat, wrapped its gauzy fingers around my leaping
lungs to remind me humans make love sounds too,

so this the first of many lessons you've taught me.
The second, that I'm too fond of illusions
of being alone. That I've taken for granted

the unbroken boundary of these sweet cream walls,
assumed that a foot of asbestos and drywall
might swallow every clamor and cum—

when I realized you were having sex, I fumbled
for my cell phone, searched for songs to drown
your lust-rattles clacking my walls, then stopped,

remembered my own bold cries shored up in silence:
arguments with my partner, late-night movie jags
until the screen glowed with the spun-gold sun,

or the time I threw up a shrimp wrap, the tail hooked
my throat's soft meat until I barked, a strangled
seal, you bore those sounds with saintly patience.

And you're the only neighbors to never use your blinds—
many nights, on the way to the dumpster or the car,
I've glanced up at the light warmed in your rooms

revered your headboard, your golden lamps, slender view
of your love-blued neck sauntered from room to room.
I've cried in need of love before.

The night after the night in blazing Charlottesville—
two days of hateful faces on my feed, voices
licked from the newsreel, a vengeful flame,

I was afraid but out of toilet paper, so I drove to Walmart
haunted by figments of hands on a torch's neck.
I cried before I ever left the lot.

I would've welcomed any display of love then.
Would've lined up in the produce aisle to watch you
bareback on the bananas, doggy on the dates,

would've cradled your love cries like a newborn,
would've nursed its miracle. Show me sweet neighbors
what it means to love loud enough for everyone,

cup the chalice of your hips, vine that ooh, baby
praise across the grapes again, the produce displays
sway in church-choir harmony—

pious plums, tomatoes unbridled and blushing,
kiwis, who turn their one emerald eye in witness,
their seeds twinkling hallelujahs in jade.

GAIA GETS DOWN AT A HOUSE PARTY
after Derrick Harriell

she live   wires in the black
light, smooth as rum sun,

she dips, births
beat, her thighs

pluck a bass line, she whistle
while she work

say *fuck it up* & she will
scorch the block hot

she got
a jaw for every pocket,

wobbles mandibles
like keys, pop-locks

her tailbone knots,
her waist's an arrow—

it obliterates. Liberate
one ass cheek

from the shorts-line
& the shoreline slates

a city. She wine
down titans—she kill

until she be killed, she
sweats & her sweat spits

wet on the backwoods,
and on the house

party—smashing space
between a stiff dick &

rhythm. She full-bodied
niggas. She twerk

& torque
          her yoke back.

WHAT GOD WANTS

god hasn't shaved her legs in a month / because god loves the body / God gave her / once god broke body for sex with a band member because he needed to believe in something / she praised him but didn't mean it / she loves her children / even when they don't know to clamp her nipple with their tongues / god wants her children to know / she is everyone else / afraid and dying / she's forgotten before she's known / she's looking for the friendless / few who understand her / another month the band member finds a better god / so god dips out watches bollywood films / she likes the gods / they give her bodies / bejeweled bedazzled dazzling / god wants her children to know she misses them most / in the dark when she cries / out the names she doesn't know / on sundays god takes church / in chicken and bubbly / the fried skin so salt of earth god is grateful / for the two friends that eat beside her / that champagne will drink / a drop of clementine and set sun-sweet / god and god and god eat / until the undone sun makes gold / of the oak tree in the yard / the same gold as gratitude

JELLYFISH BALLAD

In the watery mouth of sleep, I dream
myself a jellyfish.
Soft-bodied in a body of salt,
my chest saline with wishes

to wake and debone my useless hands,
to twist my fingers to ribbons,
to not walk—*undulate*, even if
undulate is a toothless handful

to make sparkle—I will sparkle
and shake on the ocean's hip
like a dancer's bedlah. Jellyfish catch
the first golden sip

of ocean light as lampshades.
Their dazzling flight, stars
parading from briny reef to briny
reef. Those little czars

of metamorphosis—they switch
one form for another, fan
their skirts in open ocean, slap
shut, a copper latch.

Would I alter my cells from woman
to womb child, return to lovable, too?
I should revile myself,
but I can't fight this inculpable

need to protect what's not worth
protecting. A self-love, resistant,
snaps in the synapse like the spark
between finger and nematocyst.

ELEGY FOR MY PSYCHE

You, Psyche, have been abused by every
late-night romp and one-night riding,
every sexual encounter is a unit ticking
off my vices—Ryan, the gamer whose
Dorito-leavened sweat stole my open
mouth and now, I'm a crossfire cussing,
each *fuck* cocks and bullets my clack-
ing teeth. Or Sergeant Emanuel whose
dutiful seed left me loyal to his ice cream
brands and selfie poses, to the steady
march of lime in a tonic and gin. Sweet
Ruben, who taught me to cup my tongue
and drink the rain. At least, I'm never
alone. At least, what I learned is true:
every man cradles his wit in his dick,
which Momma taught me after another

man stitched a patch on her psyche's quilt. Elegy, too, for the many men who have lost so much of themselves that they are now, like Reno, a pot of grits with no salt, an ocean with no shark, a detonator without a bomb. Imagine the Kleenex grandstanding in a gathering of junk, while women, powerful as soucouyants, suck a man clean from his bones, pour their legs like pitch around his neck, then spark—so much joy in their matchstick smiles, the bed burns.

Mami Wata

On the beachside, beer bottles glitter like tombstones
in the sand, while a man roots his thumb into coast
whiter than a waking dream. The ocean yawns. I peer
into her long, jade throat. The man finds a sand flea,
holds it for me to see its shell, bullet-round, bright
as teeth, then he chucks it in his bucket, mausoleum
for the dead he's caught. A surfboard spanks the ocean's
thigh. She lows with joy. She has seen enough of death
to barely flutter her lashes. Somewhere beneath
her lacy skirts, a legacy of bones: waving
phalanges, femurs rooted as trees, sternums clasped
on the beat of the ocean's mothering heart.
Sand fleas are not fleas. Instead, crabs spit into wet
bands of sand near the shore, returned later by mercy,
on a cold, silver hook. A casket and cradle,
the ocean crosses her legs and waits. We come back
in time. The man claps his hand around another
crab. Without looking the distance has grown between
us, so much, he seems a specter rubied with sun.
I step into the water and ocean kisses
my calves, my knees, cradles my brown, familiar feet,
then lifts the whole beach out beneath me as if she
might carry me everywhere, anywhere I ask, even home.

Love Poem for that Night We Made Salsa Verde and Learned What Capsaicin Is

Tomatillos, shucked and pearlescent with oil,
wait on the rack to roast. We chop [jalapeños]
[serranos][poblanos], declutter the clustered
seeds with our thumbs, and when the salsa's done, tuck
tortas in our prowling mouths, feed with feasting
fingers on our own sweet skin, chuck the clutter
from the countertops then [suckle][nuzzle][shovel]
a groping finger into my damp earth, unaware
of the peppers still gloving our hands. Capsaicin,
a word which here means heat, its deep roots
burrowing [the grooves of our nipping fingers] [the wetness
I give] my nerves becoming kindling for a pepper's
campfire. I [fray][scorch]. [My pink hood curls into ribbons]
[sparks spit between my lips] but you kiss the calm back
into me, search [cabinets] [baskets] [the dust-stacked rings
of Saturn] for any oil to cull the lashing
tendril of capsaicin inside me, find the tapered bottle
of olive oil then pour its blessing on my pulsing
peony, the cool green dipping like [a dancer][an anointing
a word which here means [miracle][watching Moses reach
into the burning bush, a word which here means I spread
for greasy relief and the skin silks red and sweet and new
like a [flute of sun-brewed wine] [tomato's uncut bloom]].

ODE TO MY STOMACH

I do not know how many miles
you hold inside you, the intestinal road
my dinner travels even now,
down the muscular clutch waking
like proofed dough. So ravenous, so
raucous in your rocking, every rice grain
sediment settling a shore in you. You are
honey dome. Power house. Piston
of digestion pump-pumping. You roar
with need or function. Evenings, purr—
a sated kitten sunk to stillness,
as if you never knew pain.
But we know pain. Dear delicate me,
sensitive to every sorbitol and sugar
found in milk, a single apple
is enough to end our sleep. I rest
a hand on your bubbled blubber. Organ
and orb, brown as a bosc pear,
simple slumberer. I have stared at the sands
of your stretch marks. The fingery hairs
reaching. Even your buttoned pout.
You are nothing I ask for. Still, you settle
in to stay. Unbridled me, you speak
and get exactly what you want.

FAT FUCK

I could reach into your fridge, tongue
the Häagen-Dazs, stuff its lengthy pint
into my ever-eager mouth—
that's the kind of sick bitch I am.

Tell me it's unhealthy
to view each meal as a battlefield.
Tell me to fight the fork,
or not   (it's too late now

the sweat dimpling my cheek
is grease).   Hold me,   let me coat
your coat with whatever
decadence I dress in:

pretty swine with McIntosh
turning on the spit.   The fragrant split
fruit browning my porky lips.
Feed me,

not to satisfy (impossible),
but to remind me what I cannot be
without—

what is a pig
if not unclean?   If not the ungodly

gristle buttering your teeth.

        I cannot be the only one
your teeth have torn into.

You are not the only teeth to cut
me down. My own mouth
gnashing—   finally,
the pain outside myself.

Tell me again I'm the one who eats
everything, then feed me everything
I've been given: fat fuck. moose knuckle.
flabby ass. cankles.

Tell me my belt wraps the world's waist
then beat me with it.

Still Life with fat girl, Post-Coitus

Spread over indigo light, sweat-
dimpled and satisfied, she basks

in amaretto aftermath.
Sour pit of his spit still pinched

between her teeth. She's teeth
and tit. She's tit

for tattooed dudes with god
complexes: fat girl and the shame

of her wants—perfumed
with lace, panties swinging

their tassel from the ceiling fan,
the yarn between her legs

yawns to center frame—
her eyes, predatory as a crocodile

cut a mauling jaw through the coast
at the canvas' edge, her thighs

circle her sex like a bowl of fruit. Look
how the lacework from her lingerie paints

shadows: incandescent shards,
or pinpoints of light, an embroidery

of sequins in her sweat.
She wants you to see her this way:

golden-eagled
and apex,

hip and hoof, gut
and tusk. She will not apologize

for the animal she's become
for once. Rather, rise

raw as a belt welt
swollen with breath

but breathing   so loud
no one can deny it.

On the Way Home from a Business Trip, fat girl Pulls into a McDonald's Drive-Thru in a Town She'll Never See Again

so when the attendant, anonymous in a macrocosm
of microphones, asks fat girl if that completes
her order, fat girl adds a McFlurry,
finally free

from shame's ballet in her throat.

fat girl pulls to the window and chitters
like a murmuration of starlings.
They both know fat girl can't afford this meal—

fat a currency, the nickels and dimes of a kilogram

and fat girl wealthy already—
but when the attendant hands fat girl her bag
they speak only the sticky sap of thank you-please,

and the world sweetens to soft serve.

fat girl returns to the uptick of traffic,
shucks her burger's wrapper, the crinoline slip,
reveals the golden wheel of bun beneath.

Yes, fat girl loves herself, too.   In the mirror,

fat girl sections herself into flavors.
She cups her stomach like a soy-ginger flank,
brushes her biceps and imagines the marbling

as wagyu steak.   Love, too, is hunger

fat girl sings to her steering wheel
then trowels a nail through reckless teeth,
uproots a sesame seed.

Oh, fat girl—

you are perfect in your longing.
Who hasn't wanted to be filet mignon?
To melt, in buttery love, on a belovéd tongue.

FAT GIRL CONFUSES FOOD & THERAPY, AGAIN

after Jennifer Jackson Berry

Who hasn't carved a fork
through a cut of cake and tasted
dollar store crowns, neon streamers,
wind-up toys coruscating on the rug
like confetti, tune of our skittering
shoes, fingers hooked to scoop
jam from the sandwiches, thumbs plump
as blackberries in our wild, wagging
mouths—those honeyed years
before I understood my body's struggle
against the morning's golden net.
Now, the patterned progress of neighbors
through the day's long maw,
the nearby train scrambling the tracks
hums static. My partner slabs
his tongue inside me, layers each lick
to strips of paper-mâché. I should tell him
there's no use. Instead, ink-pour
to the fridge for another bite of cake,
feel, finally, like a bird's nest, its delicate dip
of twig and twine, slip a new gown
of frosting on my tongue, hope what sugars
stays long enough to taste it.

FAT GIRL READS GREEK MYTHOLOGY ON A FRIDAY NIGHT

fat girl nurses an old book's pages,
dusty sheets rasp on her breast's cusp,
an infant. She thumbs the intimate
print, shuffles myth, the characters

stamp her landscape: Uranus at the window,
Poseidon in the bath. Gaia, naked in lamp light,
rummages through fat girl's closet, holds the low
cut dress to her chest, rubs cotton on her clavicle.

Gaia is world-wide & wild, fat girl loves her
with the tepid humidity of a mother's want.
But fat girl is all heat for the hecatoncheires:
hundred-handed ones, their fifty heads bobble

like begonias. They clatter teeth to earlobes,
they chatter and their hundred hands flap,
a bolt of cloth in an imaginary breeze.
How wonderful, fat girl imagines, to be held

by a hundred hungry hands, to have her body
bathed in a bevy of palms.
Gripped by desire, fat girl drops her book,
strokes her own skin with feasting

fingers: this is what she really wants:
to be clutched in furious love,
a hundred hands slick with self
could never be enough.

SOMETIMES FAT GIRL TAKES SHOWERS IN THE DARK
For L.H.

Earlier this year, the black hole at the center
of our galaxy blinked a record
brightest, a flash unfurling its warbler
wings, light escaped and pouring
from a clenched fist, still not as bright
as the bulbs that wheeze above my mirror,
orbiting the naked sun: my body
torched, sweat marring my under
breast, my dimpled knees, even the shadows
squeezed between my thighs. I flip the switch.
What does my body love more than tricks
of light? My body almost human
in the right mood: breasts downturned
and bashful, a smile webbed in the fat
between each hip. Or my body nature-
heavy, silver rivers stretching down
my wrists, tributaries iridescent
with fish, my back craggy with black
water. I want to praise what hides
in the dark, quasars and neutron stars
cracking into the universe like fresh eggs,
my gut, de-shaped by dark, a stubborn
spark in the hunger birthing my world.

FAT GIRL SPENDS SATURDAY ALONE, FINALLY

Hunger is not her lover, companion, mother—
just a silver edge sickling her gut. She struts
but doesn't careen into the kitchen,
a tire slinging from its rim. She'll eat
an unremarkable breakfast: one fistful
of almonds, two fistfuls of blueberries
from the carton, a mug of coffee so sweet
she could think of the first sip as the garden
scent of a treasure box carved from oak,
but she is finally alone, so she swallows
the comparison whole. Noon, showers
until steam pinks the pale parts of her toes
then lies Black, naked under the blue eye
of her TV set. She could love this
voyeurism. She could crack her glory
angles into oracle bones, her knees
and elbows forming the notch and crotch
of any language you'd want to read inside her,
but sometimes fat girl forgets to simile.
Sometimes fat girl waits for the sun to sink
on its haunches, then she goes for a walk
in her neighborhood, trees sweating,
streets heaving their tarry breath above
the rooftops, while she walks, her footsteps
don't echo or squeak, don't bullhorn or mean
anything more than fat girl was here,
she went somewhere.

fat girl is Obsessed with Jellyfish

because, as a girl, her mother took her to Myrtle Beach
in November, too cold to bloom
her girlhood in the sun or clench a happy clam
from its cradle of foam.

Instead, the two of them
wormed their toes through a half-mile of coast,
plucked coquinas from the surf, chucked sand
into the breaks between waves

and there, beside a fistful of feldspar
peppered into dirt, a jellyfish's rainbowed remains:
luminescent dew, a gelatinous porkbelly of blues
smoother than the moon's bone edge. Wider, even,
than the open-mouthed ocean. How to resist being swallowed
by tentacles? The shore crowned with gems of near-dead
cells, nematocysts barbed to protect, even, their rot.

How could fat girl resist the hunger of becoming
a woman whose hips fan like bells, whose stretch marks
flood their canals, whose vortices of stingers
circle cyclones around her neck like pearls?

FAT GIRL DANCES WITH A STRANGER AT A BLOCK PARTY

the whole hood's ascended light: bodies luminous
against the street's dark tar, girls stiletto-lifted,
a clatter of ass and brass—fat girl drops, too,
spine rattling its keys, tailbone free from the lock,
fat girl grinds on anybody who wants to learn
how to praise the ocean. They throw hands on her,
cradle her rock-a-bye hips with ritual awe,
unify—the line between a seam suturing
one sea to another. Somewhere, screams season
the August air, no more malicious than smog strung
as light's on the city's horizon. fat girl stay grindin',
joy sweltering sweat on her butterflied thighs.

fat girl Climaxes While Working Out at the Gym

I throw my legs into the stirrups of the hugging
elliptical, my knees droplet off the surface
of a hi-hat's crash while Cardi B reminds me
of my cardinal needs: a fat-sack money bag
and fat-stacked nigga, a pussy packed sweeter
than Saturday. So I kegel, cause I gotta
have one and why not pussy? Pussy's got character.
Pussy would pick up ginger ale for your stomachache
at 3 A.M. then not complain. I want pussy
caramel as palm sugar, and twice as neat.
I want my pussy to smell like gardenia. I want
my pussy to know I have loved it since the first time
I pried its smile into a lazy camera's eye,
spied its abundance of pink—the trembling lip
of a conch shell or tulip's dazed and hazy hue—
and pussy, you are the only me I've loved regardless.
I tend you with a gardener's knotted hands.
I work you while my lungs flex and clench their fists.
Because with you, pussy, I'm the baddest bitch—
a peacock spider with her fangs in another man's
throat—larynx red as a stiletto, I stab blood
from every rug I step on, and I'm strutting closer
to a near-explosion of lights, and yes,
oh yes, they must be seeing this, illuminated
in this cerebral glow, too, this flicker more holy

than Ina Garten shearing through the TV sets,
look at me—this light and lyric, this exaltation
of Cardi, the Good Book of Bardi, a Bartier
hymn hems even my toes, but no.　　No one notices.
The music galore between fat girl and Pussy
ignored. What to do with this private
love but moan some more. Pussy, we are loud
with an insistence to be. We are a nailbed cupped
with cum, a scuffle of air hoping to lung.

Notes

"Blood Ode" was written in mourning of Breonna Taylor, George Floyd, Ahmaud Arbery, and the numerous, numerous Black lives lost to police brutality. It borrows a line from Angel's Nafis' "Ode to Dalya's Bald Spot": "you ever look at a thing / you ain't make, but become /a mother in the looking?"

"Four Years After My Third-Degree Burn, My Parents Divorce" was written after Truong Tran's "scars".

The title and italicized lines in "Semi-Confessions from the Poet of Wickedness" are pulled from Walt Whitman's "Song of Myself".

The italicized line referenced in "The Last Time I Saw My Grandfather" is from Ai's "Cuba, 1962."

"Hysterectomy" is a deconstructed bop. The bop is a form developed by Afaa Michael Weaver—a poetic argument in three stanzas, each followed by a repeated line or refrain.

"Gaia Gets Down at a House Party" was inspired by the Gaia character in Derrick Harriell's *Stripper in Wonderland.*

The concept of "what god wants" is based on the following quote from Erykah Badhu's 1997 single, "On and On": "If we were made in His image / then call us by our names / Most intellects do not believe in God / but they fear us just the same."

"Mami Wata" was influenced by meditations on recovery in the wake of the middle passage. It is in conversation with the following quote by Edwidge Danticat: "[our forefathers and foremothers] too believed that the sea was the beginning and end of all things, the road to freedom and the entrance to Guinin".

"fat girl Confuses Food & Therapy, Again" is written after Jennifer Jackson Berry's "Fat Girl Confuses Food & Sex, Again".

Acknowledgements

With deep awe and admiration for the editors and staff of the following publications, in which some of the poems, and their previous iterations, in this book appeared:

BOAAT: "my ex-boyfriend is a dick joke"

Court Green: "The Last Time You Are Close to Your Body," "Ode to My Neighbors," "fat girl is Obsessed with Jellyfish"

Great River Review: "fat girl Climaxes While Working Out at the Gym"

Grist Journal: "What I Have to Give"

HEArt Online: "There's No Praise in Me for Me," "An Address to my Pain"

Limp Wrist: "Hysterectomy"

Massachusetts Review: "The Last Time I Saw My Grandfather," "Trying to Write a Music Poem"

The Missouri Review: "Blood Ode", "Breath Ode"

Nelle: "Mami Wata", previously "black girl Goes On Vacation in Orange Beach"

Ninth Letter: "Looking Out My Bedroom Window in Postignano"

The Offing: "Fat Fuck"

Pittsburgh Poetry Review: "what god wants", "Ode to My Stomach"

Sporklet: "Ode to Magic," "Stripping," "Three Lessons on the Adolescent Body"

Sixth Finch: "Sometimes fat girl Takes Showers in the Dark," "fat girl Spends Saturday Alone, Finally"

Thought Erotic: "Elegy for my Psyche," "Love Poem for the Night We Made Salsa Verde," "Still Life with fat girl, Post-Coitus"

Tupelo Quarterly: "On the Way Home from a Business Trip, fat girl Pulls into a McDonald's Drive Thru", "fat girl Confuses Food & Therapy, Again"

This book was a self-discovering, self-building process. It was a process that needed a vast network of support. And with that, some thank yous are in order.

So first, thank God.

Thank my partner, Wesley—who doesn't "get" poetry but still sat with me through every poem, every draft, ever hour spent pacing over language and for that I have never felt so understood.

Thank my family for understanding I am healing. To my parents, Mary and Edward, for their prayers and pep talks. For my little sister Anaise, who is as much an inspiration as a source of solace. Thank you.

Thank you, godmother. Thank you, godfather. Thank you aunts, uncles, cuzzos and them.

Thank you, Henry Israeli, Christopher Salerno, Rebecca Lauren Gidjunis, Jake Bauer, Robin Vuchnich, and the entire Saturnalia Books team.

Thank you, Patricia Smith, for believing in what this book had to say. Thank you Donika Kelly and L. Lamar Wilson for your infinite kindness and generosity. Thank you for being the voices that helped me carry this book into the world.

Thank you, Diana Kitthajaroenchai and Lauren Buchness, for your breath-taking art.

Thank you to my UWG friends and family. Thank you to the faculty and administrations at The University of Alabama and Florida State University, which funded my graduate study. Thank you, Barbara and Lamar, for your mentorship in these spaces.

Thank you for support from the April 26th Foundation. Thank you to the faculties and fellows at the Callaloo Creative Writing Program and the

Tin House Summer Writers Workshop. Thank you to the organizers and participants of the Convivio Conference.

Thank you to all my dear friends and to the friends who had direct influence on this book—Nabila Lovelace, Kelsey Fleming, Katie Taylor, Lauren Howton, Camille Adams, Melissa Clairjeune, Mallary Rawls, Kayleb Candrilli, Jennifer Jackson Berry, Jessica Rae Bergamino, Rachel Wiley, Yolanda Franklin, Natalie Lima, Misha Benjamin, Kidd Monstar, and Jasmine Glenn. Thank you to the dear friends who influenced this book by influencing my heart.

And to all the fat girls, the Black girls, the fam just tryna make it—I see you. We outchea. We thrivin'.

Mother Body is printed in Adobe Garamond Pro.
www.saturnaliabooks.org